GEORGE TICE

SELECTED PHOTOGRAPHS

D1219953

"Golden Boy"

AT&T, Basking Ridge, New Jersey, 1999

GEORGE TICE

SELECTED PHOTOGRAPHS

1953 — 1999

℗

A POCKET PARAGON BOOK

DAVID R. GODINE · PUBLISHER

BOSTON

A Godine Pocket Paragon
first published in 2001 by
David R. Godine, *Publisher*
Post Office Box 450
Jaffrey, New Hampshire 03452
www.godine.com

Copyright © 2001 by George Tice

Library of Congress Cataloging-in-Publication Data
Tice, George A.
George Tice : Selected Photographs, 1953-1999 — 1st ed.
p. cm. — (Pocket paragon)
isbn: 1–56792–153–1 (softcover : alk. paper)
1. Photography, Artistic. 2. Tice, George A. I. Title. II. Series.
TR654.T522   2001
799'.092—dc21   00–061713

PAGE 1: Sailboat · *New Jersey, 1962*
OPPOSITE: Ice Series #9 · *Clark, New Jersey, 1967*

First Edition

Printed in Shenzhen, China

To the memory of Lee D. Witkin
He made photography his cause

WATER TOWER · *Rahway, New Jersey, 1994*

FOREWORD

The eighty photographs by George Tice carefully reproduced in this Pocket Paragon have been selected from forty-six years of dedicated and intensive work by one of this country's great talents. From his 1953 image, *On the Bowery*, to his *Golden Boy* of 1999, his is a career that spans the last half of the twentieth century, starting at age fourteen with the purchase of a $29.95 Kodak camera, and progressing unabated through the beginning of this century. Although his achievements have been rewarded by a dozen published books, innumerable one-man exhibitions, and countless awards, it is only recently that his reputation has shifted from that of "master printer" (and there are precious few who possess the skills necessary to match his exquisite silver prints or his complete understanding of the techniques demanded by the palladium and platinum processes) to "master photographer," an honorific this book should fully confirm.

Tice's interests are as immediately identifiable as his images. They are profoundly American in their reach and scope, and they are especially attuned to his native state of New Jersey, where his ancestors first settled ten generations ago, where he was born in Newark in 1938, and where he has lived most of his life. Occasionally, his work takes him farther afield, as in his search for Lincoln, or to the hometowns of quintessential Americans like Ronald Reagan, Mark Twain, and James Dean, or to the nearly extinct Shakers of Sabbathday lake, the rugged coast of Maine, the Amish country of Lancaster County, Pennsylvania, and the cold, windy moors of Yorkshire, England. Tice once commented, "If I were given the choice of traveling to China or Missouri, I'd probably pick Missouri. I want to be known as an American photographer." Much, we could add, as another self-effacing New Jerseyan, the poet William Carlos Williams, wanted to be known as an "American poet," an observer and recorder of our vernacular territory who instinctively knew that "some common memento is better" than the more rarefied "hothouse flowers."

What makes Tice so instantly recognizable as a photographer is more than his subject matter. He has the uncanny ability to see, and indelibly record, the monumental embedded in the ordinary. The image can be of a water tower in Rahway, like some futuristic machinery out of H. G. Wells, looming over the tangled patterns of an ancient tree, the brilliant, almost surreal, radiance of a crenellated White Castle diner, gleaming in the night like a whitewashed medieval castle, the innocent swagger of two Amish boys returning from school, or a mountain stream in Vermont.

A second aspect of these photographs that seems striking is the almost prenatural *stillness* they possess. Tice has a genius for stopping movements *and* moments in time, for creating a certain majesty of stasis and silence. It is possible that this is simply the result of a large lens and long exposures, but so many of these images appear to seat themselves securely in both space *and* time, to define a moment both in terms of its action and its mass.

A brief word might be in order about how small books like this are conceived and published. In many respects, the organization and sequencing of small format books are more difficult than larger "coffee-table" extravaganzas. The margins are tighter; space is at a premium; every image has to tell. Here, too, Tice has proven himself a thorough professional. Nothing in the sequence, sizing, or juxtaposition of these photographs is capricious or accidental. Tice has personally assembled enough books to realize that the viewer is generally looking at a spread, at two images that must interact and complement each other. Also, that photography books, just like novels, short stories, and books of poetry, have to maintain their own internal rhythms; they should carry the reader along at a pace that is, with luck, determined by the creator, not by the whims of the reader.

In the seventeenth century, the historian Joseph Moxon described the duties and responsibilities of the complete typographer. If you substitute photographer for typographer, you will understand the scope of abilities Tice brings to his art: "By a typographer, I mean such a one who, by his own Judgement, from solid reasoning with himself, can either perform, or direct others to perform, from the beginning to the end, all the Handy-work and Physical Operations relating to Typographie." Unlike many of his contemporaries, Tice has the ability, indeed the determination, to control *all* the aspects of his craft. Be they pictures of Bodie, Paterson, or Ticetown, the images presented in this book display his craft as well as his extraordinary vision of everyday life, all meticulously composed & scrupulously printed. Like most great artists, Tice has the ability to make us look closely, to transform the mundane into the memorable, and in doing so, to reveal, irrevocably and often apocalyptically, the inherent nobility of his subjects.

George Tice will probably never be a celebrity; bragging and showmanship, strident ostentation and the need for personal publicity are anathema to the core of his personality. He is an artist who lives for and through his work, and his work is all the testimony we really require to know the man. His photographs, in their own quiet and understated way, manage to say more about America, where it has been and where it is going, than the work of any person I know.

— DAVID R. GODINE

On the Bowery · *New York, 1953*

CORN CRIB · *Chester, New Jersey, 1955*

OLD WOMAN AND BOY · *Shelby County, Tennessee, 1958*

ABOARD THE "MEMPHIS QUEEN" · *Memphis, Tennessee, 1958*

14

KITTY · *Memphis, Tennessee, 1958*

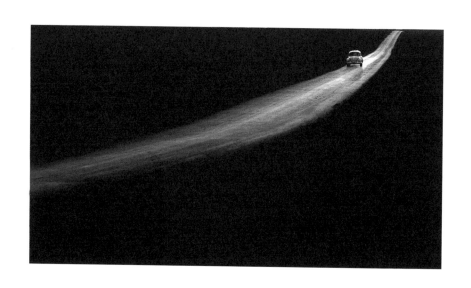

COUNTRY ROAD · *Lancaster, Pennsylvania, 1961*

VILLAGE OF EAST CORINTH · *Vermont, 1963*

MARIE · *Pennsylvania, 1960*

PICNIC ON GARRET MOUNTAIN · *Paterson, New Jersey, 1968*

LYNN · *Rahway, New Jersey, 1966*

FROM THE CHRYSLER BUILDING · *New York, 1978*

SUNRISE · *New York, 1971*

BUGGY AND FARMHOUSE WITH WINDMILL · *Lancaster, Pennsylvania, 1965*

HAYFORK · *Lancaster, Pennsylvania, 1968*

OLD AMISH MEN · *Lancaster, Pennsylvania, 1966*

Two Amish Boys · *Lancaster, Pennsylvania, 1962*

AMISH CHILDREN PLAYING IN SNOW · *Lancaster, Pennsylvania, 1969*

Wagon and Buildings · *Bodie, California, 1965*

TOMBSTONE · *Bodie, California, 1965*

CAIN HOUSE AND METHODIST CHURCH · *Bodie, California, 1965*

TREE #22 · *California, 1965*

Aquatic Plants #1 · *Saddle River, New Jersey, 1967*

OAK TREE · *Holmdel, New Jersey, 1970*

FERNS · *Peckamoose, New York, 1971*

WATERFALL · *Peckamoose, New York, 1971*

MOUNTAIN STREAM · *Manchester, Vermont, 1970*

GORGE · *Peekamoose, New York, 1971*

SHAKER INTERIOR · *Sabbathday Lake, Maine, 1971*

MR. AND MRS. ALVAH THOMPSON · *Port Clyde, Maine, 1971*

PORCH · *Monhegan Island, Maine, 1971*

KEENAN'S BARBER SHOP · *Portland, Maine, 1971*

46

CLOTHESLINE · *Monhegan Island, Maine, 1971*

TREE WITH CARVINGS · *Paterson, New Jersey, 1967*

CAR FOR SALE · *Paterson, New Jersey, 1969*

THE PASSAIC FALLS · *Paterson, New Jersey, 1968*

HOUSE ON FRANKLIN STREET · *Paterson, New Jersey, 1967*

JOE'S BARBER SHOP · *Paterson, New Jersey, 1970*

53

FERRY SLIP · *Jersey City, New Jersey, 1979*

PETIT'S MOBIL STATION · *Cherry Hill, New Jersey, 1974*

CHARLIE AND VIOLET · *Jersey City, New Jersey, 1979*

56

WHITE CASTLE, ROUTE #1 · *Rahway, New Jersey, 1973*

STRAND THEATER · *Keyport, New Jersey, 1973*

NATIONAL FUEL OIL COMPANY · *East Newark, New Jersey, 1973*

ARTIE VAN BLARCUM · *North Arlington, New Jersey, 1975*

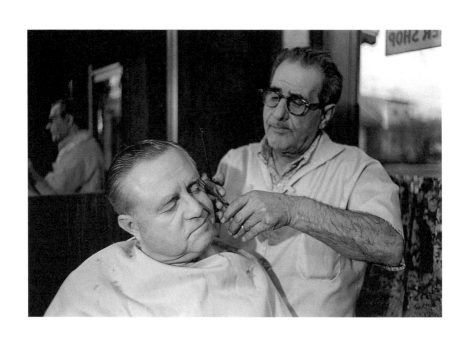

ARTIE VAN BLARCUM · *North Arlington, New Jersey, 1977*

ARTIE VAN BLARCUM · *Grassy Sounds, New Jersey, 1975*

DEBORAH · *Iselin, New Jersey, 1978*

DEBORAH · *Manasquan, New Jersey, 1978*

DEBORAH · *Iselin, New Jersey, 1978*

Deborah · *Iselin, New Jersey, 1978*

WHITE CAT SERIES · *Iselin, New Jersey, 1978*

WHITE CAT SERIES · *Iselin New Jersey, 1978*

WHITE CAT SERIES · *Iselin, New Jersey, 1980*

STREET CORNER, TALLINN, ESTONIA · U.S.S.R., 1983

LINCOLN · *Newark, New Jersey, 1981*

LINCOLN · *Chicago, Illinois, 1982*

LINCOLN · *Cleveland, Ohio, 1981*

WINSLOW FARM · *Fairmount, Indiana, 1985*

JAMES DEAN'S MOTORCYCLE · *Fairmount, Indiana, 1985*

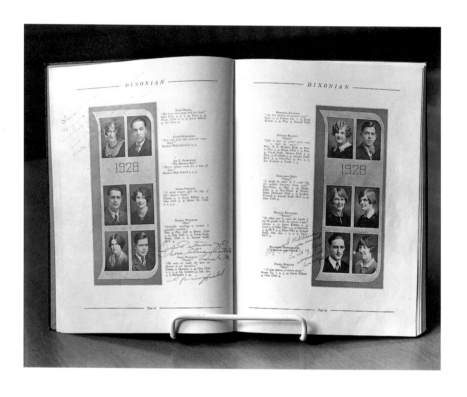

FIRST STREET COIN WASH · *Dixon, Illinois, 1985*

SHOP WINDOW · *Hannibal, Missouri, 1987*

LEO COOPER · *Hannibal, Missouri, 1984*

BUCKSTONES, SCAMMONDEN MOOR · *Yorkshire, 1990*

EN ROUTE TO WHITBY · *Yorkshire, 1990*

JACK ROBINSON'S BAROMETER, DENHOLME GATE · *Yorkshire, 1992*

FORTUNE TELLER, WHITBY · *Yorkshire, 1990*

STAIRWAY TO WHITBY ABBEY · *Yorkshire, 1990*

OLD TRACTOR · *Ticetown, New Jersey, 1992*

APPLE BLOSSOMS · *Ticetown, New Jersey, 1994*

FALLEN APPLES · *Ticetown, New Jersey, 1994*

THE HOMESTEAD · *Ticetown, New Jersey, 1994*

WRECKED BOAT · *Morgan, New Jersey, 1993*

COLOPHON

GEORGE TICE: SELECTED PHOTOGRAPHS, 1953–1999 was set in Zapf Renaissance Book, the work of the acclaimed type designer, calligrapher, and book designer, Hermann Zapf. The display type is Michelangelo, also a Zapf design. Both faces clearly reveal their roots in calligraphic tradition, and the Renaissance italic has a particularly lively rhythm. The book was printed in 200 line-screen duotone on Monadnock Dulcet paper by C & C Offset Printing Company Limited.

Designed by George Tice and Jean Elizabeth Poli
Composition by Carl W. Scarbrough

BOOKS BY GEORGE TICE

FIELDS OF PEACE
A Pennsylvania German Album
(with Millen Brand)

GOODBYE, RIVER, GOODBYE
(with George Mendoza)

PATERSON

SEACOAST MAINE
People and Places
(with Martin Dibner)

GEORGE A. TICE
Photographs 1953–1973

URBAN LANDSCAPES
A New Jersey Portrait

ARTIE VAN BLARCUM
An Extended Portrait

URBAN ROMANTIC
The Photographs of George Tice

LINCOLN

HOMETOWNS
An American Pilgrimage

STONE WALLS, GREY SKIES
A Vision of Yorkshire